Looking for Common Ground on U.S. Trade Policy

A publication of the
CSIS International Business Infrastructure Initiative

Author
Murray Weidenbaum

Foreword by
Erik R. Peterson

August 2001

About CSIS

For four decades, the Center for Strategic and International Studies (CSIS) has been dedicated to providing world leaders with strategic insights on—and policy solutions to—current and emerging global issues.

CSIS is led by John J. Hamre, formerly deputy secretary of defense, who became president and CEO in April 2000. It is guided by a board of trustees chaired by former senator Sam Nunn and consisting of prominent individuals from both the public and private sectors.

The CSIS staff of 190 researchers and support staff focus primarily on three subject areas. First, CSIS addresses the full spectrum of new challenges to national and international security. Second, it maintains resident experts on all of the world's major geographical regions. Third, it is committed to helping to develop new methods of governance for the global age; to this end, CSIS has programs on technology and public policy, international trade and finance, and energy.

Headquartered in Washington, D.C., CSIS is private, bipartisan, and tax-exempt. CSIS does not take specific policy positions; accordingly, all views expressed in this publication should be understood to be solely those of the author(s).

Cover Photo Credit

Digital Imagery
© copyright 2001 PhotoDisc, Inc.

Library of Congress Cataloging-in-Publication Data
CIP information available on request

ISBN 0-89206-405-6

The CSIS Press
Center for Strategic and International Studies
1800 K Street, N.W., Washington, D.C. 20006
Telephone: (202) 887-0200
Fax: (202) 775-3199
E-mail: books@csis.org
Web site: http://www.csis.org/

Contents

Foreword   iv

Preface   vi

1   Introduction   1

2   Economic Background   5

3   The Major Criticisms of the Global Economy   9

4   Examining the Major Criticisms   10

     Are Imports Hurting Americans?

     Are U.S. Companies Running Away, Especially to Low-Cost Areas Overseas?

     Is the United States a Free Trade Patsy?

     Are We Ignoring the People Hurt By Globalization?

     What Is the Case for Labor and Environmental Standards?

     Is There a Role for Voluntary Standards?

5   Identifying Common Ground   25

     Ways to Increase the Benefits of Trade Policy

     Ways to Reduce the Costs of Trade Policy

About the Author   30

Foreword

In the highly charged political environment surrounding trade policy, few individuals have confronted firsthand the policy challenges associated with the many complex forces at work. Even fewer have demonstrated the capacity to take the "strategic" perspective—to assess the respective positions constructively without focusing on the bumper-sticker rhetoric and sloganeering that all too often seize the headlines. And fewer still have the determination to hunt for common ground well after others have surrendered to the notion that such common ground cannot or does not exist.

Murray Weidenbaum is one of those rare individuals. His extensive leadership experience in public service has already spanned three decades, starting with his tenure at the Treasury Department, marked by his chairmanship of the Council of Economic Advisers in 1981–1982, and manifesting itself most recently in his chairmanship of the U.S. Trade Deficit Review Commission. In these and other capacities, Murray has developed a remarkable "long view" of trade policy. He has been on the frontlines as positions have evolved, perceptions changed, tactics shifted, and policies formulated in the range of groups and individuals involved in the formulation of trade policy. Moreover, owing to his unique experience in the worlds of government, business, and academia, Murray has demonstrated the capacity to go beyond the mere "optics" and focus on the real underlying positions, the genuine reservation points, and the concrete areas in which consensus can be built.

In light of this background, it is no surprise that Murray is now dedicating himself to analysis on how we can find common ground in trade policy. As an academic at Washington University, as Mallinckrodt Distinguished University Professor, he has contributed significantly to the intellectual underpinnings of the policy debate. As chairman of the Trade Deficit Review Commission, which among other things highlighted how divided Americans are on the issue of trade policy, he saw firsthand how profound and deep-seated the conflicts really are.

But it is encouraging that such a knowledgeable and seasoned observer persists with the notion that gaps can be bridged, new approaches can be formulated, and new solutions devised—all guided by the goal, as Murray argues, of "expanding the benefits of trade and reducing the costs in ways that do not imperil the benefits."

As this publication was going to press, U.S. Trade Representative Robert Zoellick and his EU counterpart Pascal Lamy argued in a jointly written *Washington Post* article that they hoped "to remove the stain of the failed Seattle talks and help launch a new round of international trade negotiations."[1] That is no small task. To

---

1. Pascal Lamy and Robert B. Zoellick, "In the Next Round," *Washington Post*, July 17, 2001, p. A17.

move into the next round, they will need to deliver their respective constituencies, build a stronger and lasting consensus for continued liberalization, maintain the common agenda that they have devised, and then translate their positions into policies that the rest of the world can accept. But as Lamy and Zoellick warn in their article, "The price for failure would be painfully high."

As titanic as these challenges are, perhaps the most significant obstacle these and other policymakers will encounter is removing "the stain of Seattle," which to many represented an inflection point at which the longstanding consensus on trade policy both in the United States and elsewhere seemed to collapse. The goal of progressive liberalization in trade was already complicated enough. But Seattle marked the superimposition of a whole new strain of virulent opposition—some legitimate, some irrational—on the phenomenon of globalization.

The first step is to take a dispassionate and careful accounting of where things are, what the trade-offs are, what the long-term implications could be, and what can be done to bring together well-meaning and constructive parties in rebuilding an approach to trade. In this report, Murray succeeds in advancing such an architecture. His writing here is an effort to bridge divergent positions at a critical time in trade policy.

We are proud that Murray is now with CSIS on sabbatical as "Distinguished Senior Adviser" through the end of the calendar year. But we are prouder still of Murray's longstanding association with CSIS—as intellectual adviser, as cochairman of the Center's International Research Council, as member of the CSIS Board of Trustees, and as friend to the CSIS community at large.

This report is the first in a series of publications that CSIS will issue as part of its initiative on international business infrastructure—an assessment of the international conditions under which the private sector now operates.

Erik R. Peterson
Senior Vice President and Director of Studies
William A. Schreyer Chair in Global Analysis
CSIS
August 1, 2001

Preface

The author is a visiting scholar at the Center for Strategic and International Studies, on leave from Washington University in St. Louis. The research for this report was begun at Rice University where the author was the Ken Lay-Vinson and Elkins visiting scholar at the Jones Graduate School of Management. An earlier version was presented at the Baker Institute for Public Policy at Rice University.

The author is indebted to many people at CSIS, especially Sherman Katz, holder of the Scholl Chair in International Business, and Sidney Weintraub, holder of the Simon Chair in Political Economy, for numerous helpful suggestions, and Aaron Moburg-Jones, an intern at CSIS, who provided very diligent assistance.

Introduction

Trade policy in the United States is at a standstill. Both Democratic and Republican administrations have experienced great difficulty in getting Congress to authorize major trade legislation. That legislative deadlock will likely endure until basic policy issues are resolved—particularly the knotty problems surrounding labor and environmental standards.

What can be done? The instinctive response in Washington, D.C., is to work up some deals—give a little to each of the most vocal advocates, notably steel and textiles, as well as labor and the environmentalists. Eventually, of course, some deals will have to be made if any legislative action is to occur at all. But first, let us get some understanding of how this deadlock in trade policy arose. Then let us start the difficult process of bridging the gap between the proponents of free trade and the opposition.

The shattering of the open trade consensus did not occur overnight. For much of the twentieth century, Americans generally supported a policy of removing barriers to international commerce and encouraging a freer flow of trade and investment among nations. During the heyday of this broad agreement, support for free trade extended from union leaders such as Walter Reuther, president of the United Auto Workers Union, to most business organizations and to consumer groups such as the League of Women Voters. Consumer Union sued, albeit unsuccessfully, to block President Richard Nixon's effort to negotiate "voluntary" reductions in steel imports. The consumer organization stated that the restriction of steel supplies would hurt U.S. consumers.[1]

During the period immediately following the end of World War II, and concurrent with American dominance in the world economy, the policy of opening trade channels provided a wide array of benefits to the American people. The signs of general prosperity were numerous. In the 1950s, for example, economic growth was high (averaging 4 percent a year), inflation was low by then-current standards (a yearly average of 2.6 percent), and unemployment (at 4.4 percent) was far below the depression levels of the 1930s. The AFL-CIO endorsed the Trade Expansion Act of 1962, which authorized the landmark tariff reductions known as the Kennedy Round. By the end of that decade, however, the AFL-CIO had moved into the camp of trade restriction. The United Auto Workers continued to support free trade for a few more years.[2]

---

1. Consumer Union, Inc. v. Kissinger, United States Court of Appeals for the District of Columbia. 506 F. 2nd 136 (1975).

2. I. M. Destler and Peter J. Balint, *The New Politics of American Trade* (Washington, D.C.: Institute for International Economics, 1999), p. 15.

By the 1970s, the broad consensus on trade policy was unraveling. Specific domestic industries, notably steel and automobiles, began to suffer the adverse effects of rising foreign competition. For some sectors of the society, unemployment was no longer just a seasonal or even cyclical phenomenon. Rather, it became a pervasive and enduring experience for many factory workers. That was especially so for those who felt they were too old to start over again in new occupations in different industries where they would be competing against younger people with substantially more education and training. The long-term unemployed tended to suffer in relative silence and the membership of the industrial unions—the United Auto Workers, the United Steel Workers, and the International Association of Machinists—declined steadily and substantially.

During the 1970s and also in the 1980s, a very different group of Americans was increasingly making its influence felt in the national media and in the political process—the environmental movement. The environmentalists surely did not suffer in silence. A wide range of Americans supported their increasingly vocal concerns about pollution and other ecological damage to the planet. Environmental activists were widely perceived as the "good guys in the white hats." Their efforts were successful in terms of the enactment of an impressive array of environmental statutes—the Clean Air Act, the Clean Water Act, the Endangered Species Act, the Toxic Substances Control Act, the Safe Drinking Water Act, Superfund, and the Resources Conservation and Recovery Act.

Much of the time, the environmental and labor movements were antagonistic to each other. Union members ridiculed the elitism of the ecology-minded and highly educated professionals, whom they construed to be out of touch with the needs and problems of the working people. The animosity was frequently reciprocated with derogatory comments about "hard hats."

A fundamental change occurred in the 1990s, slowly at first. Both environmental and labor leaders perceived that their key opponent was the same—the business community. Business wanted more access for trade and investment in foreign markets; labor and greens sought measures to raise working and environmental conditions in those markets. The unions and some environmental groups worked together, albeit unsuccessfully, in opposing the North American Free Trade Agreement (NAFTA). They did succeed, however, in achieving some "side agreements" which made environmental and labor standards a part of the ongoing debate on international trade policy.

A more technical but no less strategic debate focused on renewing the president's "fast-track" authority to negotiate trade agreements on which the Congress would be required to take an up-or-down vote, with limited opportunity for amendments. Here major labor and environmental groups (but not all of the latter) joined forces in opposition to granting President Clinton the fast-track authority that had become standard in the international trade area since the presidency of Gerald Ford—unless that authority specifically included as objectives the negotiation of labor and environmental standards. To the surprise of many in the free trade camp, who had underestimated the strength of the opposition, the fast-track legislation was defeated. Since 1994, therefore, the president has lacked this authority.

In the fall of 1999, labor, environmental groups, and others worked together in a highly visible and dramatic fashion, marching in the streets of Seattle in opposition to the priorities, policies, and procedures of the World Trade Organization (WTO). The WTO trade ministers were then meeting in an effort to plan negotiations on a new round of trade agreements. For a variety of reasons, including key disagreements between the developed and developing nations as well as the disruption caused by the marchers, the WTO meetings in Seattle concluded in failure.

Many issues other than the traditional debate over free trade versus protectionism have arisen to accentuate the cleavage between the business focus on economic factors and the "public interest groups" that emphasize such social concerns as human rights and biotech foods, as well as labor and environmental standards. Most of the latter groups focused on what they considered to be the excessive power of corporations, personified by large multinational enterprises. This antipathy to private business ironically coincided with unparalleled national success on the economic front. Business groups responded by noting the unusually strong performance of the U.S. economy and tried to take much of the credit.

Yet, rather than broadening the support for open trade, the expansion of income and wealth exacerbated the bitterness of those who felt left out of the broad-based prosperity. Moreover, the widespread accumulation of substantial wealth enabled some people of means to finance attacks on the perceived shortcomings of the economic system, especially in the environmental area.

Also, the rise of an extremely large trade deficit was taken by some observers as an indication that something was fundamentally wrong in American trade policy. Although so far those unprecedented trade deficits have been readily financed by foreign investments, a view that the economy is increasingly vulnerable to a "hard landing" has gained some credence. That could occur if foreign investors suddenly reduced or halted their investments in the United States and maybe even pulled out of some of their existing holdings—with adverse effects on the dollar, U.S. financial markets, and the level of economic activity. This was not the prevailing view among professional economists, who tended to see the large U.S. trade deficit as mainly the by-product of American prosperity.

Nevertheless, many interest groups also considered the large trade deficits to be evidence of unfair treatment through denial of market access by the countries that Americans traded with, especially Japan and China. They were not convinced by the writings of the great majority of professional economists who viewed protectionist policies of our trading partners as mainly affecting the geographic and product distribution of the trade deficit, but not its size. Such "theoretical" consideration did not receive much attention in more "practical" debates on trade policy. Moreover, many of the opponents of open trade were more concerned about the imports that affected them directly, regardless of the magnitude and even the direction of the overall trade deficit.

The contending groups, who saw the trade deficit from different perspectives, experienced increasing difficulty in communicating with each other, much less were they able to achieve agreement on basic issues. The growing disparity of views was brought home in the years 1999–2000 in the workings of the U.S. Trade Deficit Review Commission. That bipartisan, blue-ribbon commission was established by

Congress with the expectation that it would help develop a consensus on dealing with the problems arising from the cluster of issues involving the trade deficit, imports, and globalization.

At the outset, the commission tried to write a single, unified report. The members elected one of the Republican appointees (the author of this report) as chairman and one of the Democratic appointees (the president of the Levy Institute of Bard College) as vice chairman. After approximately a year and a half of joint effort, however, a split report was issued. Only four of the seven chapters were signed by all members of the commission, the most important being the chapter on helping the workers displaced by trade. The issue of labor standards was one that could not be resolved. Yet, it does not necessarily evoke the spirit of Pollyanna to conclude from this mixed experience that, with substantial further effort, a basis could be developed for identifying common ground on which both sides of the international trade debate might eventually agree.

The rising public concern about the people being left behind during periods of economic progress requires going beyond the customary response—teach the public about the benefits of free trade. Such efforts at economic education certainly are in order, but they do not suffice. A more positive and activist approach must extend beyond merely providing information; it must deal with the costs as well as the benefits of trade policy. In that spirit, this report is organized around the dual notion of expanding the benefits of trade and reducing the costs in ways that do not imperil the benefits. A basic starting assumption is that U.S. policy on international trade must evolve from the traditional approach if it is to be successful in the years ahead and get off of dead center.

This task requires identifying some common interests on the part of groups who have developed very different ways of looking at the economy and its relation to the larger society. On the one hand, there are enthusiastic supporters of open markets who see private enterprises generating faster economic growth, better working conditions, and the rising living standards that are conducive to more democratic governments. However, at the same time, many other individuals and organizations believe with equal force that globalization is responsible for abuses of human and labor rights and of the environment, while undermining the culture and sovereignty of nations. The task of reconciliation is complicated by the fact that there is both truth and overstatement in each of these two viewpoints.

CHAPTER 2

Economic Background

Some brief economic background may be in order. International trade is more important to the United States today than at any time in the past, both in absolute terms and in relation to the size of the economy. Each minute of each day, approximately $2 million worth of goods and services are exported by U.S. businesses and a bit over $2 million of goods and services are imported. These traded items are integral parts of our economy—exports of wheat, airplanes, and professional services and imports of oil, minerals, clothing and consumer electronics. Overseas customers buy more than one-half of our annual production of computers, cotton, aircraft, and soybeans; more than one-third of our construction machinery, semiconductors, and machine tools; and over one-fourth of our farm machinery, flat glass, and corn. Economic studies show that the jobs that trade creates pay better wages, provide greater benefits, and offer more security than jobs not connected to trade.[3]

By dollar value and volume, the United States is the world's most important trading nation. We are the largest importer, exporter, foreign investor, and host to foreign investment. The United States is indeed a vital part of that global marketplace, which, increasingly, affects so many U.S. workers, managers, investors, and consumers.

It is, however, far more than a matter of the expansion of the quantity of international commerce. A basic qualitative transformation is occurring, which can be summed up as "globalization." Globalization is an ongoing process that more closely integrates the many local, regional, and national markets for goods, services, capital, and information. This process has been accelerating in recent years, especially in broadening the reach of competitive forces. That faster pace has been made possible by reductions in government barriers to trade and investment plus technological innovations in transportation and communication that substantially diminish the relevance of distance for business transactions.

More than a trillion dollars move effortlessly around the world each day. Effective and low-cost telecommunication is the pacing element. The cost of a three-minute phone call from New York City to London dropped from $245 in 1920 to $9 in 1950 to 78 cents in 1999. During the same period, the cost of air travel declined from 68 cents a passenger mile to 12 cents.[4] Advances in shipping and transportation have thus made it possible for a company to deliver a product to most places in the world overnight and for people to travel long distances at relatively low cost.

---

3. U.S. Trade Deficit Review Commission, *The Trade Deficit* (Washington, D.C.: U.S. Government Printing Office, 2000), pp. 123–124.

4. Murray Weidenbaum, *Business and Government in the Global Marketplace*, Sixth Edition (Upper Saddle River, N.J.: Prentice-Hall, 1999), p. 187.

Although globalization has not made national borders irrelevant to commerce, these boundaries are not as important as they were 20 or 30 years ago in determining the location and organization of production and employment. Globalization has broad implications—positive and negative—for people, businesses, and governments. People now have greater access to a wider array of goods and services, many of them at much lower prices than were available a generation ago. Perhaps even more important, people have easier access to information. It has become more difficult for hitherto closed societies to wall off information that encourages political reform while continuing to permit the dissemination of information that promotes economic activity.

Of course there are still a lot of poor people in the world who do not participate in the progress that has been made, but contrary to many critics, globalization has reduced that number. In 1990, 450 million people in East Asia subsisted on less than $1 a day. By 1998, the number was estimated at less than 280 million.[5] Wars, natural disasters, totalitarian governments, pervasive corruption, mismanagement, and anarchy all share the blame for the remaining abysmal poverty.

At the other end of the income distribution, substantial progress has occurred in the United States, although poverty (measured on a very different scale) has not been eliminated. In recent years, incomes of the poorest families rose at the same pace or even a little faster than those of the wealthiest. From 1993 to 1998, the real incomes of the poorest 20 percent of families increased at an average of 2.7 percent a year, while the top 20 percent averaged gains of 2.4 percent annually.[6]

Perhaps the best measure of the benefit of globalization is the relationship between international trade and economic growth. Between 1960 and the early 1990s, the economies of countries that exported small proportions of their output grew less than 3 percent a year. In contrast, countries exporting large proportions of their production averaged growth rates of 5–7 percent a year.[7] The process is more complex, however, than merely shipping goods and services overseas. To gain from open markets, countries must offer political stability, sound economic management, and educated workers—characteristics also essential to their domestic success. Around the world, these key attributes of economic freedom equate with a higher living standard. In 1997, the per capita income of the most economically free nations averaged over $18,000, against just $1,700 for the least free.[8]

Nevertheless, the effects of globalization are not all so benign. A more open economy also means that Americans face new challenges and opportunities both in the marketplace and in the workplace. Globalization is breaking down the barriers between different markets, including barriers that should shield businesses and workers from competition. That means that consumers benefit from the fact that

5. *World Development Indicators 2000* (Washington, D.C.: World Bank, 2000), tables 4.10 and 4.11.

6. John M. Berry, "This Time, Boom Benefits the Poor," *Washington Post*, February 14, 2000, p. C5.

7. Dennis Rondnelli and Jack Behrman, "The Promise and Pains of Globalization," *Global Focus*, vol. 12, no. 1 (2000), p. 6.

8. James Gwartney and Robert Lawson, *Economic Freedom of the World: 2000 Annual Report* (Vancouver: Fraser Institute, 2000), p. 15.

most items that can now be traded can be produced in the most efficient location for sale in almost any market. However, internationalization of the marketplace also means that businesses as well as workers feel the effects of competitive forces from around the world—and far more quickly than in the past.

Workers are under pressure to improve their skills and productivity to take advantage of the opportunities presented by globalization and to avoid becoming economically obsolete. For businesses, globalization increases the need to seek lower costs and higher quality in production. That can mean "outsourcing" more work to suppliers, increasing reliance on production in offshore facilities, and making greater use of technological innovations.

Governments also experience the effects of the challenges of globalization in many ways. For the United States, with increased international integration of financial and product markets, the nation is ever more closely linked with other economies, including some whose political systems, macroeconomic policies, business practices, values, and cultures differ greatly from ours. One challenge to the U.S. government is to promote common "rules of economic engagement" that are clearly understood and supported in international commerce around the globe.

While globalization has changed the role of national governments and the importance of geographic boundaries in business decisions, rumors of the demise of national borders as a factor in world trade are greatly exaggerated. Public-sector influences on trade and capital flows have been substantially reduced but not eliminated. Subsidization of some domestic industries continues, both at home and abroad. Government-imposed restrictions are the most evident, but not the only, remaining barriers. International transactions involve exchange rate risk, which is not a factor in domestic business. Differences among national tax systems also affect business decisions on locating production and distribution facilities. The public concerns, however, are far more fundamental than these important technical factors.

According to recent public opinion polls, most Americans worry that, while international trade does generate benefits, there is a serious downside. In particular, a widespread view holds that trade costs U.S. jobs, that low-paid foreign workers making products imported into the United States displace better-paid U.S. workers. The political debate over "free trade" versus "fair trade" overlays this concern, leading some to believe that the United States does not gain from trade as much as other nations do, particularly those that do not play by the same rules.

One recent survey of public opinion captures these ambivalent views:

Overall, Americans see globalization as somewhat more positive than negative and appear to be growing more positive about it. A large majority favors moving with the process of globalization and only a small minority favors resisting it...

In principle, a majority of Americans supports the growth of international trade, especially when the removal of trade barriers is clearly reciprocal. However, Americans are lukewarm about the actual net benefits of trade to most sectors of society, except for the business community. A majority believes trade widens the gap between rich and poor. A strong majority feels trade has not grown in a way that adequately incorporates concerns for American workers, international labor standards and the environment... .[9]

An underlying reason for this ambivalence is the rising sense of insecurity among U.S. workers, notwithstanding the historically low rate of current unemployment. Despite a national unemployment rate in the neighborhood of 4.5 percent, the percentage of workers who fear they will lose their jobs is three times higher today than at the height of the 1981–1982 recession when the unemployment rate rose above 10 percent.[10] Further, while wages for college-educated workers have been rising steadily, wages for those with a high school education or less have been stagnant for most of the last two decades—although the most recent statistics indicate there was some real growth in these wages in the latter half of the 1990s. Many other factors, primarily rapid technological change, have been blamed for the wage stagnation suffered by less-skilled workers, but the most visible are globalization and imports.

Resentment has increased on the part of workers who believe that they are forced to compete against the exploited labor forces of the poor, developing nations whose cost of production is much lower than in the United States. This feeling of unfairness is fed by the belief that many job opportunities are lost because other nations dump their surplus products on our markets below cost and simultaneously restrict the opportunity for American companies to export into their markets. At the same time, however, many developing countries as well as some industrial nations consider Americans to be overbearing and too domineering in international economic relations. An indication of the difficulty of dealing with trade issues is that the United States can be viewed simultaneously as both an easy mark and as a bully.

Let us take up each of the major concerns, while trying to avoid the position of a debater scoring easy points. Attempting to respond to the public's serious worries in a constructive manner may illuminate a path for developing a new international trade policy for the United States. As will be seen in the following section, these issues are more complex than generally realized, with important considerations brought up by each side of these controversies. We should be mindful of the warning of economist Dani Rodrik that, if these issues are not managed "intelligently and creatively," the domestic consensus in favor of open markets will ultimately erode.[11]

9. Program on International Policy Attitudes, School of Public Policy, University of Maryland, *Americans on Globalization* (College Park, Md.: University of Maryland, 2000).

10. Mishel J. Bernstein and J. Schmitt, *State of Working America, 2000–2001* (Ithaca, N.Y.: Cornell University Press, 2001), p. 24. See also Jay Mazur, "Labor's New Internationalism," *Foreign Affairs*, January/February 2000, pp. 79–93.

11. Dani Rodrik, *Has Globalization Gone Too Far?* (Washington, D.C.: Institute for International Economics, 1997), p. 6.

CHAPTER 3

The Major Criticisms of the Global Economy

We can group the various criticisms of current U.S. policy on international trade into five major categories.[12]

1. *Unfair imports are hurting Americans, and our government is asleep at the switch.* The major argument is that hard-working people are losing their jobs because foreign products are being dumped in the U.S. market below the cost of production. Plant closings and downsizing are seen as becoming the rule, while U.S. companies respond to this situation by running away to low-cost areas overseas.

2. *Other countries treat the United States as a patsy because we are an idealistic island of free trade in a cynical world of protectionism.* U.S. exports are not treated fairly by the countries that export so freely to the United States.

3. *The people hurt by globalization are being ignored while the winners are enjoying all the benefits.* As a result, the United States is becoming an unfair and more unequal society.

4. *Labor, environmental, and human rights standards are being overlooked in the rush to invest in low-cost production abroad.* The NAFTA side agreements on labor and the environment are a fig leaf and ineffective. The International Labor Organization (ILO), which is supposed to deal with many of these matters, is a paper tiger. To underscore the problem, there is no counterpart agency for the environment.

5. *At the same time, the developing countries see us as a bully.* In their view, we are using our political and economic power to impose expensive Western standards on their poor economies. According to their officials, all our moralizing and posturing is a disguise for an insidious protectionist effort to keep their products out of our markets.

That is quite a litany of complaints. We should not hesitate to correct the inaccuracies and exaggerations imbedded in these criticisms. But that is not a satisfactory response. In order to revive the lost momentum in international trade policy, it is necessary to deal with the real problems that underlie and motivate these charges. The following section undertakes that difficult assignment.

---

12. This section is a distillation of the hearings held by the U.S. Trade Deficit Review Commission in 1999–2000. (See CD-ROM accompanying *The Trade Deficit*.)

CHAPTER 4

Examining the Major Criticisms

Let us now examine and respond to the major criticisms of the global economy and of U.S. policy.

Are Imports Hurting Americans?

The myth that imports are bad per se will be quickly recognized by students of economics as the mercantilist approach discredited by Adam Smith over two centuries ago. The fact is that the nation benefits from imports in many ways (which is not to say that everyone benefits from trade or from any other policy). Consumers get access to a wider array of goods and services. Domestic companies obtain lower cost components and thus are more competitive. We get access to vital metals and minerals not found in the United States. Also, imports prod our own producers to improve productivity and invest in developing new technology.

Every car owner has seen the quality of domestic automobiles improve in the 1980s and 1990s because of foreign competition. A striking example of the broader benefits of imports occurred more recently. In 1997–1998, the expanded flow of lower-cost products from Asia kept inflation in the United States low at a time when the Federal Reserve would otherwise likely have been raising interest rates to maintain price stability. If the Fed had to adopt a tighter monetary policy in those years, the result would have been a weaker economy. Moreover, in a full-employment economy, imports enable the American people to enjoy a higher living standard than would be possible if sales were limited to domestic production.

The special importance of imports was highlighted recently by the director of the Washington State Council on International Trade: "The people who benefit most critically are families at the lower end of the wage scale who have school-age children and those elderly who must live frugally." She went on to conclude: "It is a cruel deception that an open system of free trade is not good for working people."[13] Nevertheless, the argument that "trade costs jobs" resonates powerfully with rank-and-file union members. They have seen one side, the downside, of the trade equation—plant closings and downsizing in the face of increased imports of textiles, apparel, steel, automobiles, and consumer electronics. They can be expected to ignore the benefits achieved by other members of society, even if in the aggregate those benefits are far greater than the costs they are suffering. At times, the indirect benefits of trade to factory workers may be greater than they realize. For example,

---

13. Testimony of Patricia Davis, director of the Washington State Council on International Trade, in Trade Deficit Review Commission, *The Trade Deficit*, p. 123.

more steel imports reduce the cost of producing automobiles and machinery in the United States and enhance the competitiveness of those U.S. products.

In any event, one sensible action-oriented response to the concerns over imports is to enforce more effectively the trade agreements the United States has entered into and to take more seriously the statutes on the books that are designed to deal with unfair import competition. This, however, is treacherous ground. At times there is a fine line between keeping out blatantly improper imports (e.g., those made by forced child labor) and merely responding to pressures to exclude products that sell at prices lower than the cost of production in the United States.

An especially knotty problem is the controversial antidumping process. It is ostensibly designed to deal with the problem of unfair "surges" of imports. However, the requirements to prove "dumping" are very low. Actions that are quite legal and customary in the United States, such as clearance sales, run afoul of the antidumping law when they involve imports. No time limit is set for starting a case, and there is no provision for a broader review of antidumping decisions initially made in a narrow sector context.

Of course, the domestic industries that benefit from keeping out competition via the antidumping process do not have many qualms about the U.S. consumer being forced, as a result, to pay higher prices. However, a new wrinkle has developed in recent years. Other nations, tired of unsuccessful negotiations on this topic with the United States, have resorted to promulgating antidumping statutes of their own. Increasingly, U.S. exporters are on the receiving end of arbitrary antidumping actions by developing countries, as well as by other nations.

Having initiated this practice, it is hard for the United States to convince other governments not to follow our precedent. We, as well as the nations we trade with, would on balance be better off if the antidumping statutes were repealed. In the case of the United States, there are other ways of dealing with "unfair" surges of imports, notably the more carefully written "escape clause," which authorizes the president to grant temporary relief to industries to facilitate their adjustment to import competition. As noted a little later in this section, an effective response to import competition is to do a better job of educating and training Americans in the skills that increase their competitiveness.

We also need to improve the understanding on the part of the American public of the full range of effects of international trade. In our interconnected economy, most of the jobs "lost" from imports are quickly replaced by jobs elsewhere in the economy—either in export industries or in companies selling domestically. The sharp run-up in U.S. imports in recent years paralleled the rapid growth in U.S. employment. That was no coincidence. Both trends reflected the underlying health of the economy. The U.S. job miracle continues to be the envy of the rest of the world. The facts are clear: as of mid-2001, U.S. employment is at a record high and unemployment is near a 30-year low. Between 1993 and 2000, the United States created more than 20 million new jobs, far more than Western Europe and Japan combined. Contrary to a widely held view, most of those new jobs pay well, often better than the average for existing jobs.

That being said, it is harder to lay off or fire a worker in Western Europe or Japan than in the United States. At first blush, that sounds like a pro-worker attitude. However, that different approach to firing workers helps to explain why employers in those countries are so much more reluctant to hire new workers than is the case in the United States. On balance, the U.S. worker is much better off.

The harsh truth is that, in good times as well as bad, some people lose their jobs. But most researchers who have studied this question conclude that, in the typical case, technological progress—not international trade—is the main reason old jobs become obsolete.[14] Moreover, at the same time far more new jobs are created.

Domestic macroeconomic policies—especially monetary, tax, and budget actions—have the greatest influence on the overall level of economic activity in the United States. In comparison, international trade is peripheral, at the most shifting the composition of jobs from low-skilled to higher-skilled occupations. In effect, the sons of shoemakers are aerospace mechanics and their granddaughters are computer analysts. Nevertheless, not everyone makes that adjustment painlessly or even successfully. How to deal with that important subject is covered later in this section.

Because many of the critics of current trade policy focus on the role of multinational corporations, it is useful to examine the factual information on their imports as well as exports. In 1997 (the latest year for which comprehensive Commerce Department numbers are available), U.S.-based multinational enterprises exported $364 billion of manufactured goods and imported $228 billion, for a positive trade balance of $136 billion. In the same year, foreign-based multinationals doing business in the United States generated an excess of $122 billion of imports over exports. U.S. multinationals typically use their foreign subsidiaries, primarily in Europe and Japan, to assemble and distribute exports from their home plants in the United States. In a similar fashion, foreign multinationals use their U.S. subsidiaries to assemble and distribute in the United States imports from their home country.

It is ironic to note the uncoordinated responses to this bifurcated phenomenon in this country. U.S.-based multinational enterprises—which by and large generate excesses of exports—are under assault here at home for their overseas operations. In striking contrast, states and localities compete against each other with all sorts of subsidies for the location of foreign-based multinationals—which usually report substantial excesses of imports.

---

14. David Blanchflower, "Globalization and the Labor Market" (paper commissioned by the Trade Deficit Review Commission, June 1, 2000), pp. 30–46. (See CD-ROM accompanying *The Trade Deficit*.) See also Ajit K. Ghose, "Trade Liberalization, Employment, and Global Inequality," *International Labour Review*, vol. 139, no. 3 (2000), pp. 303–304.

Are U.S. Companies Running Away, Especially to Low-Cost Areas Overseas?

The critics seem to have the direction wrong. The flow of money to buy and operate factories and other businesses is overwhelmingly into the United States. This country has not experienced a net outflow of investment since the 1960s. That is the flip side of the trade deficit. Financing large trade deficits means that far more investment capital comes into this country than is leaving.

But let us examine the pattern of the overseas investments that are made by U.S. companies. The largest proportion (an average of 68 percent in the decade of the 1990s) goes not to poor countries, but to the most developed nations, those with high labor costs and high environmental standards. The primary motive is to gain access to markets. That is not too surprising when we consider that the people in the most industrially advanced nations are the best customers for sophisticated U.S. products. By the way, only one-third of the exports by the foreign branches of U.S. companies goes to the United States. Almost 70 percent goes to other markets, primarily to the industrialized nations.

Turning to U.S. investments in Mexico, China, and other developing countries, the result often is to enhance U.S. domestic competitiveness and job opportunities. This is so because many of these overseas factories provide low-cost components and material to U.S.-based producers who are thus able to raise, or maintain, their international market shares. The attractiveness of these countries as investment locations is confirmed by the most recent data. Foreign affiliates of U.S. firms are expanding more rapidly in the developing nations. During the period 1989–1998, the developing nations' share of U.S. foreign-affiliate manufacturing employment rose from 33 percent to 41 percent.[15] The knotty subject of labor and environmental standards for these overseas locations is covered a little later in this report.

Is the United States a Free Trade Patsy?

Do other nations erect trade barriers? Of course they do, and we should not ignore them, although the trend has been to cut back these obstacles to commerce. But the United States's hands are not as clean as we like to think. U.S. import barriers come in many shapes, sizes, and varieties, including the following:

- Buy American laws give preference in government procurement to domestic producers. Taxpayers pay the higher costs that often result.

- The Jones Act prohibits foreign ships from engaging in waterborne commerce between U.S. ports. That is why cruise ships to Alaska (which usually are U.S.-owned but registered in foreign countries with less regulation) start in Vancouver, Canada, rather than in Seattle.

---

15. Joseph P. Quinlan and Andrea L. Prochniak, "The Global Downsizing of Corporate America," *Morgan Stanley Dean Witter Global Insights*, January 24, 2001, p. 2.

■ Many statutes limit the import of specific agricultural and manufactured products, ranging from sugar to pillowcases.

■ Tariffs on specific items, notably textiles, can be quite high.

■ State and local regulatory barriers, such as building codes, aim at protecting domestic producers—rather than taxpayers or consumers.

These barriers to trade, however, are ultimately disappointing. Nations open to trade grow faster than those that are closed.[16] Nevertheless, foreign trade barriers and unfair treatment of U.S. products competing in foreign markets offend the sense of fairness of Americans who see the greater openness of our economy. In areas where the United States often has a comparative advantage, notably trademarks and copyrights on new products, property rights are frequently violated in countries that lack a strong legal system and enforcement tradition.

For example, imitation Bausch & Lomb Ray Ban sunglasses are sold in China as "Ran Bans." The packaging of Kellogg's Corn Flakes is mimicked on boxes of "Kongalu Corn Strips" by means of identical type fonts and color layout and the use of the widely recognized Kellogg rooster. Lux soap knockoffs are marketed as "Lix" or "Lud." Often Asian counterfeiters produce identical copies of Western technology with little if any delay. Taped copies of the hit movie *The Lion King* were sold in Beijing before the film's official release on videotape in the United States.

China's enforcement in the main has been in the form of crackdowns on the politically weak street vendors, and rarely on the far more important factories that mass produce the counterfeit copies. In the relatively few instances when the major producers are closed down—with considerable publicity—they are quietly reopened when attention shifts to another issue.[17]

Although trade barriers do not affect the size of a nation's trade deficit (or surplus), the companies and workers affected cannot be expected to take solace in the knowledge that the benefits to others are greater than the hurt they are experiencing. It surely is consistent to match the professional economists' antipathy toward trade barriers at home with at least equal opposition to foreign restrictions on commerce. A comprehensive policy to break down trade barriers, at home and abroad, is in order.

As a general proposition, it seems appropriate that the United States should embark on a policy to fully enforce the trade agreements—especially the market-opening ones—that this nation has entered into. A companion effort is needed to ensure that the nations we trade with fully enforce the agreements that they have entered into.

This requires increasing the modest enforcement resources now devoted to these purposes. The U.S. Department of Commerce unit charged with monitoring compliance with trade agreements should be expanded. The size of its China office declined from 8 officers to 4 between fiscal years 1992 and 1999, Western European officers from 31 to 18, and its Japan office from 17 to 8.[18] These cutbacks occurred

16. Jeffrey Sachs and Andrew Warner, "Economic Reform and the Process of Global Integration," *Brookings Papers on Economic Activity*, 1996, no. 1, p. 36.

17. Ibid., p. 170.

despite substantial growth in U.S. trade with those nations. Given the increased number of trade agreements that the department monitors and enforces and the large number of disputes with major trading partner, the modest staff expansions in the last several years are not adequate.

We also need to recognize our own barriers to our exports. For national security and public policy reasons, the United States restricts potential exports but the distinction between military and commercial products is becoming increasingly blurred. A rising share of the military budget goes for communications, imaging, and data processing—all of which are areas of accelerated commercial activity. Also, to keep costs down, the armed services are increasingly using standard commercial products. Cutting off from the world marketplace the American companies that provide these products to customers in other nations attenuates our ability to innovate and to keep up with overseas competitors.

As for sanctions unilaterally preventing Americans from doing business with a nation to which our foreign policy leaders want to "send a message," there is little if any evidence that such sanctions work. U.S. business, labor, and agriculture are harmed for what is merely a symbolic gesture.

Are We Ignoring the People Hurt By Globalization?

An initial, but incomplete, answer to the question is a simple, "no." The federal government maintains a substantial social safety net for people who have lost their jobs. The general safety net includes unemployment compensation, food stamps, and a scaled-back welfare program plus a variety of tax benefits, especially the earned-income allowance (a form of negative income tax).

For those hurt by imports, trade adjustment assistance is provided, including extended unemployment compensation, job search help, relocation expenses, and training support. A larger package of benefits is provided for those adversely affected by NAFTA. The latter also covers those who had worked in companies supplying the factories directly affected by imports from Canada and Mexico or which relocated to either of those countries.

The basic rationale for government involvement in trade adjustment is that fairness requires those who benefit from government policies to help those who bear the costs. As a practical matter, the people hurt by imports—even those who just think they are adversely affected—can be expected to take a less generous view of the global marketplace than those who are the beneficiaries. If the losers believe they are being ignored while the rest of the society benefits at their expense, resentment will surely increase generating strong political pressures for protectionism. This is exactly the dangerous process that is occurring today.

Formulating good international economic policy does not mean trying to redistribute the pain of those who are hurt by change. A return to protectionism would create a new set of winners and losers—and the winners would not likely be in the majority. The need is to help those who are hurt by trade without doing far greater

---

18. Trade Deficit Review Commission, *The Trade Deficit*, p. 222.

harm to those who benefit. Such a constructive approach requires increasing the extent to which our fellow citizens participate in the economic growth generated by an open international economy. A similar conclusion was reached in an important report on the benefits of trade by the Organization for Economic Cooperation and Development (OECD). The OECD stated firmly, "… we must respond to the concerns of those citizens who are—or who perceive themselves to be—adversely affected by … trade … ."[19]

The most fundamental aspect of an effective adjustment policy is to do a much better job of educating and training Americans to become more productive and higher-wage members of the nation's workforce. A more productive labor force, in turn, is the key to long-term international competitiveness.

Nevertheless, trade adjustment assistance remains a controversial area of labor policy. Some think that the government does too much, encouraging people to delay returning to work. Others believe that the government does too little to help people who are hurt by trade. Still others see a host of bureaucratic inefficiencies and shortcomings in the assistance programs.

The initial answer suggested here is not to increase the budgets for the existing adjustment efforts, although that could well be part of the long-term solution. Such action is premature, however, until the existing deficiencies are identified and corrected. Numerous bureaucratic obstacles face the beneficiaries of the ongoing trade adjustment training programs. For example, the duration of unemployment compensation does not cover the full period of eligibility for training. The older Trade Adjustment Assistance Program and the newer NAFTA adjustment program are not well coordinated. The potential beneficiaries complain about the complexity of the rules (which helps to explain the relatively small number of participants).

Labor market experts note that the most important factor in a successful worker adjustment program is the speed of the assistance. Minimizing the length of time between being laid off and getting assistance is crucial. The longer that people are unemployed, the more likely that potential employers will discount their qualifications. The current system has built-in delays. Trade adjustment benefits do not begin until after the unemployed worker has exhausted the initial half year of unemployment benefits.

The following suggestions for improvement were made in a recent survey of state unemployment offices:

1. Income assistance should be provided for two years if workers need remedial education as well as training (many apparently require both to qualify for new jobs).

2. The regular Trade Adjustment Assistance Program and the special one for NAFTA should be mandatory partners in a one-stop delivery system. One access point should be established for employment-related and training services at which job search and assistance services are also available.

3. Better yet, the two trade adjustment programs should be consolidated and their disparate rules and regulations unified and simplified.[20]

---

19. *Open Markets Matter: The Benefits of Trade and Investment* (Paris: OECD, 1998), p. 4.

So far, however, economists have found little evidence that trade adjustment or other government-sponsored training works. A comprehensive study financed by the Trade Adjustment Assistance Program concluded that the training it finances fails to produce a positive impact on earnings, at least during the first three years after the job loss. This finding supports the skepticism that many unemployed workers show toward additional education or classroom training. On the other hand, job search assistance, particularly if it gets underway promptly, can speed up reemployment, especially if the worker is rusty in terms of knowing how to locate and apply for a new job. Relatively low-cost job search assistance is effective in shortening the length of time that participants need to receive benefits.[21]

Most workers displaced by trade eventually find new jobs, but the burden on the workers and their communities can be high. Those new jobs are often in lower-paying industries at lower wages with less benefits. On average, workers lose about 16 percent of their earnings in a new job following a job loss, and a quarter of the workers with health insurance lose their coverage. For older workers, in particular, the poor prospects of finding a job with close to comparable earnings and benefits can lead to permanently dropping out of the work force.[22]

All this provides incentive for pursuing new ways of helping displaced workers find good jobs. As noted earlier, rapid technological change is the most important reason for the elimination of old jobs—as well as the creation of new ones. This underscores the need to enhance the job skills of the workers who are displaced from traditional, low-tech industries. Among overlooked approaches is a larger role for junior or community colleges. Many of the 1100 community-oriented institutions of learning are now organized especially to help displaced workers, including those who need to brush up on their basic language and math skills.

In some cases, community colleges help people launch new businesses, especially in areas where traditional manufacturing is declining. Thus, losing a job can lead sometimes to a basically new career, especially with some temporary assistance. Hazard Community College in eastern Kentucky, for example, has taken on the mission of helping displaced coal miners start their own businesses. In its first four years, the college helped launch 145 new small businesses, each providing an average of four new jobs.[23]

20. Trade Deficit Review Commission, *The Trade Deficit*, pp. 165–166.

21. Paul Decker and Walter Corson, "International Trade and Worker Displacement," *Industrial and Labor Relations Trade Review*, vol. 48, July 1995, pp. 758–774; Leah E. Marcal "Does Trade Adjustment Assistance Help Displaced Workers," *Contemporary Economic Policy*, vol. 19, no. 1, January 2001, pp. 59–72.

22. Gary Burtless, Robert Z. Lawrence, Robert E. Litan, and Robert J. Shapiro, *Globaphobia* (Washington, D.C.: Brookings, 1998), pp. 143–145.

23. Trade Deficit Review Commission, *The Trade Deficit*, p. 170.

What Is the Case for Labor and Environmental Standards?

One of the most controversial aspects of international trade policy—perhaps the single most divisive issue at the present time—is the proposal to make trade agreements contingent on adopting international standards on labor and the environment. At first blush, the notion that the process of negotiating agreements to open international trade provides a fine opportunity to improve the social conditions in the developing nations sounds like a high-minded way of doing good. After all, who is not in favor of a cleaner environment and raising the living standards of poor countries?

The situation is far more complicated than it may seem at first, however. To begin with, developing countries generally oppose with great vehemence the imposition on their national sovereignty of what they see as unaffordable Western standards. They fear that Western-dominated organizations will wind up determining African standards for paying textile workers and telling Asian countries how much to spend on toxic waste treatment. The developing economies see the imposition of costly labor and environmental standards as a disguised way of keeping their low-cost products out of the markets of the advanced, developed nations. *New York Times* columnist Thomas L. Friedman labels these standards "politically correct protectionism." This cynical attitude was conveyed by Youssef Boutros-Ghali, Egypt's trade minister, "Why, all of a sudden, when Third World labor has proved to be competitive, do industrial countries start feeling concerned about our workers?"[24]

Those suspicions were reinforced by the strong union opposition to the recent congressional action giving duty-free access to some U.S. apparel markets to the products of the poorest African countries. The labor union opposition was maintained *despite* the linkage of higher worker standards in the African trade bill. The measure was enacted over the protestations of the unions.[25]

Not surprisingly, business generally has opposed the linkage of trade and social standards as a costly interference with open markets. That may sound hard hearted and motivated by self-interest, which undoubtedly is the case. However, the results of imposing arbitrary standards on very poor developing countries can be very different than anticipated by the human rights and other groups supporting such standards. For example, soon after a bill was proposed in Congress in 1993 to ban imports from countries where children work in factories, garment makers in Bangladesh fired an estimated 36,000 workers under the age of 18. Studies by the ILO and Unicef found that few of the fired workers ended up in school. Apparently, many took more-dangerous jobs or became prostitutes.[26]

The benefits of eliminating child labor may not be as great to impoverished families in Asia as they may seem to comfortable Americans. It is hard for many

---

24. Quoted in David E. Sanger, "A Grand Trade Bargain," *Foreign Affairs*, January/February 2001, pp. 66–67.

25. Thomas L. Friedman, "Parsing the Protests," *New York Times*, April 14, 2000, p. A31.

26. Pete Engardo, "Global Capitalism," *Business Week*, November 6, 2000, p. 76.

citizens of Western nations to understand the kind of conditions that prevail, for example, in Cambodia. According to the Associated Press, abject poverty is driving some families to sell their babies to orphanages for as little as $12. A broader study published by the ILO noted that "Family survival of poor households often depends on children's work."[27]

Some insight into the cynical response of many developing nations to apparent Western idealism can be attained by examining our own history. As recently as 1918, the minimum age for child labor in North Carolina was 12. Indeed, in that year, the U.S. Supreme Court invalidated congressional action to institute a national minimum of 14 years.[28]

Nevertheless the effort to link social standards with trade agreements has developed strong support in the United States. Considerable movement in public policy in this direction has occurred. Labor standards have been recognized as a relevant issue in several major trade laws, even though precise linkage was not required.

- The 1984 amendments to the Trade Act of 1974 provided that the extension of trade preference for developing countries contain a provision to deny those benefits to any country that "has not taken or is not taking steps to afford internationally recognized worker rights to workers in the country." However, the president can waive this provision "in the international economic interests of the United States."

- The Omnibus Trade and Competitiveness Act of 1988, authorizing U.S. participation in the Uruguay round of trade talks, included "worker rights" as the fourteenth of 16 principal trade negotiation objectives, but the law did not require that the trade agreement necessarily had to incorporate specific standards.

- The 1994 law implementing the results of the Uruguay round called upon the president to "seek the establishment in … the WTO of a working party to examine the relationship of internationally recognized worker rights to the existing international trade regime." (That issue was one of the items that contributed to the deadlock in trade discussions at the Seattle WTO meeting in December 1999.)

- The legislation establishing NAFTA set up commissions on labor cooperation and on environmental cooperation.[29]

- Article XX of the General Agreement on Tariffs and Trade (the forerunner of the WTO) allows countries to ban imports of goods produced using prison labor so long as the bans are not a form of disguised protectionism.

---

27. Chris Decherd, "Starving Cambodians Sell Babies," *Houston Chronicle*, February 11, 2001, p. 11A; Richard Anker, "The Economics of Child Labour," *International Labour Review*, vol. 139, no. 3 (2000), p. 259.

28. Michael S. Greve, *Laboratories of Democracy: Anatomy of a Metaphor* (Washington D.C.: American Enterprise Institute, 2001), p. 4.

29. Destler and Balint, *The New Politics*, pp. 22–23. The two commissions have been criticized for lack of accomplishment.

- The 1999 agreement with Cambodia, reducing U.S. tariffs on most imports from that country from 17 percent to 4 percent. In addition to complying with a new labor law that sets forth basic rules for health and safety on the factory floor, Cambodia also pledged to follow the core ILO labor standards.[30]

- The completed (signed in October 2000, but not yet congressionally approved) U.S.-Jordan Free Trade Agreement includes new language on labor rights: "The parties shall strive to ensure that such labor principles [referring to the ILO Declaration on Fundamental Principles and Rights at Work] and the internationally recognized labor rights … are recognized and protected by domestic laws." The agreement also provides for monetary fines, rather than trade sanctions, as punishment for violating these provisions.[31] (Labor unions support the agreement as an important precedent; however, the Business Roundtable, the leading group of corporate chief executives, refused to back the agreement in a split vote in February 2001.)

- The presidents of 33 Western Hemisphere nations, meeting in Quebec in April 2001, pledged to start a Free Trade Agreement of the Americas (FTAA) by 2006. President George W. Bush stated that he would proceed only if the agreement were combined with "a strong commitment to protecting our environment and improving labor standards."[32]

Under the circumstances, it is appropriate to examine the ILO labor standards and the process by which such standards are adopted. In 1998, the ILO adopted four "core" labor standards, which have been referenced in a variety of American and foreign trade discussions:

1. Freedom of association and the effective recognition of the right to collective bargaining;

2. Freedom from forced labor;

3. The effective abolition of child labor; and

4. Nondiscrimination in employment.

Of all the international organizations, the ILO is unique in having equal representation from business, labor, and government, and a history of research and international agreements that extends to the period before World War II. Most nations, including the United States, are members. Thus, the ILO would seem to be the proper place to take up the issue of international labor standards, and many have urged that course of action. Indeed, the first WTO ministerial-based confer-

---

30. Wayne, Arnold, "Translating Union into Khmer," *New York Times,* July 12, 2001, p. C1 *et ff.*

31. *Agreement Between the United States of America and the Hashemite Kingdom of Jordan on the Establishment of a Free Trade Area,* October 25, 2000. See also Kimberly Elliot "Fining our way on trade and labor standards?" *International Economic Policy Briefs,* IIE DC PB01-5, April 2001, pp. 1–5.

32. "A Cautious Yes to Pan-American Trade," *The Economist,* April 28, 2001, p. 35. The president of Brazil indicated that he would only support the agreement if it includes changes in U.S. antidumping rules.

ence, in 1996, adopted a resolution declaring that the ILO is the appropriate place to take up labor standards.

The ILO has serious shortcomings, however. Over the years it has earned a reputation for setting high-minded goals but not following up with adequate action. This is especially true with regard to promoting high labor standards in developing nations. Part of the problem is of our own doing. Congress has ratified very few of the ILO's "conventions" (13 out of 183) and only 2 out of 4 "core" standards.[33]

The ILO will not be taken more seriously until the major industrialized nations, especially the United States, provide the resources and the support to demonstrate that the ILO is indeed the proper forum to deal with international labor standards. As a practical matter, the United States is very limited, at the present time, in its use of the ILO as an enforcement mechanism for such standards because it can only initiate complaints with respect to agreements that it has ratified. Ironically, this country has adopted and enforced internal labor standards that equal and often exceed ILO's. A very substantial body of labor rules has been established by such federal regulatory agencies as the Equal Employment Opportunity Commission, the Occupational Safety and Health Administration, the National Labor Relations Board, the Office of Federal Contract Compliance, the Pension Benefit Guaranty Corporation, the Labor Department's Wage and Hour Division, as well as the Internal Revenue Service.[34]

In contrast, the WTO has no experience or expertise in enforcing international labor standards and has expressed no interest in taking on such a role. It would seem to make good sense for the United States to promote a realistic alternative by leading a vigorous effort to strengthen the effectiveness of the ILO. Merely opposing the WTO as the place to take up international labor standards will not suffice.

One suggestion for broadening the role of the ILO is to publicize, especially through the Internet, the instances where countries violate the core standards. This approach would enable consumers in various nations to vote with their dollars whether or not to punish countries with substandard working conditions.[35] A global survey of 22,000 consumers in early 2001 revealed that 20 percent of respondents had taken some action in the past year to "punish" companies that were known to violate human and labor rights.[36]

In May 2001, China announced a pioneering program of cooperation with the ILO. According to the new agreement, the ILO will provide advice on workplace safety, collective bargaining, and labor disputes. As the first project under the new cooperative program, Switzerland provided $1.9 million for an effort to improve labor-management relations and human-resource policies in companies in Shanghai, Chongqing, and Dalian.[37]

---

33. Destler and Balint, *The New Politics*, p. 23. See also Kimberly Ann Elliott, "Getting Beyond No... ," in Jeffrey Schott, *The WTO After Seattle* (Washington, D.C.: Institute for International Economics, 2000), pp. 187–204.

34. See Weidenbaum, *Business and Government in the Global Marketplace*, chapters 5 and 6.

35. Robert E. Litan, "Trade Policy: What Next?" *Brookings Review*, Fall 2000, p. 43.

36. Report by the Millennium Poll on Corporate Responsibility, conducted by Environics International Ltd. See "Consumers Punishing Abusive Companies," *USA Today Magazine*, April 2001, p. 16.

In the absence of a counterpart to the ILO in the environment area, not many positive alternatives to direct linkage with trade agreements have surfaced. One of the few such suggestions has been made by a trade expert who believes that the WTO cannot become an environmental organization. Jeffrey Schott urges that the trading rules be made more environmentally friendly. The range of GATT Article XX exceptions (recall the provision authorizing trading nations to keep out products of forced labor) could be expanded to provide "safe harbors" for trade actions consistent with provisions of specific multilateral environmental agreements. Thus, the United States and other nations could be allowed to truly protect endangered species, but not on a unilateral basis.[38]

In 1996, the WTO Committee on Trade and the Environment seemed to indicate that WTO rules would permit member nations to exclude imports made in ways that violated an environmental agreement, provided that the agreement allows for such actions and that both the offending nation and the responding nation are parties to the agreement. In the same year, a WTO appeals panel indicated that GATT Article XX could be interpreted to permit WTO members to exclude imports under a multilateral environmental agreement.[39]

Is There a Role for Voluntary Standards?

There is a third possibility between the polar alternatives of compulsory international labor and environmental standards and reliance on the traditional workings of the marketplace. It is the voluntary actions by individual companies that seek to give their overseas management guidance and direction on labor and environmental matters.

A number of large U.S. producers and distributors of consumer goods made in whole or in part in developing countries have been setting their own operating standards. Often responding to domestic pressures, these companies have established specific rules and enforcement procedures for their overseas operations. While governments continue debating the subject, apparel producers such as Nike, Reebok, and Levi Straus have joined the Fair Labor Association. This private organization is gearing up to launch an inspection program covering overseas factories. The object is to see to it that designated minimum labor standards are adhered to—such as a ban on child labor and ensuring that workers are paid at least the legal minimum wage by the suppliers to the member companies.[40]

The toy producer, Mattel Company, adopted its Global Manufacturing Principles unilaterally in 1997. The principles govern its factories and vendors worldwide. They require workers to be paid at least the applicable minimum wage or a wage

37. Erick Eckholm, "China Accepts U.N. Advice To Help Labor Strife," *New York Times*, May 20, 2001, p. 5.

38. Jeffrey Schott, "The WTO After Seattle," in Schott, *The WTO*, p. 28.

39. Peter Morici, *Labor Standards in the Global Trading System* (Washington, D.C.: Economic Strategy Institute, 2001), pp. 17–18.

40. Joseph Pereira, "Apparel Makers Back New Labor Inspection Group," *Wall Street Journal*, April 10, 2001, p. B1 *et ff.*

that meets local standards, whichever is higher. No one under the age of 16 or the local legal age limit (whichever is higher) may work in a factory that produces products for the company. Mattel also pledges not to use suppliers employing forced or prison labor. The company's environmental, health, and safety standards are based on those of the American Conference of Government Industrial Hygienists.

Because of skepticism about the enforcement of these standards, Mattel set up an Independent Monitoring Council. The council audits the factories of the company and its suppliers to assure compliance with the manufacturing principles. It has discretion to make its findings public. The council's work is augmented by auditors from PriceWaterhouseCooper, who inspect payroll records, and a team of interviewers from a nongovernmental organization, Verité. The latter holds confidential one-on-one meetings with hundreds of employees. The council checks on whether the audited plants are in compliance with country laws and Mattel's principles. The audit process covers a variety of potential problems such as inadequate ventilation, chemical odors, excessive variation in in-plant temperatures, and inadequate use of safety equipment. It also verifies that the workers are paid according to the official pay structure.[41]

The members of the independent monitoring council sponsored by Mattel believe that the independently monitored voluntary approach is superior to compulsory standards (the author is a member of the council):

> ... a system of standards voluntarily created and implemented is the preferred way to achieve progress in these areas of public and private policy. We do not believe that a system of government-mandated global standards is either desirable or sustainable. Worldwide trade and production systems involve a great variety of products and services, labor markets, competitive conditions, and changing technologies. To subject all these to uniform standards, or to create regulations that attempt to foresee all possible situations and provide detailed rules for their handling, would make the system inordinately onerous, bureaucratic, expensive, and ultimately unworkable.[42]

As would be expected, some critics are unhappy with the voluntary nature of corporate standards and are suspicious of the adequacy of their enforcement. A balanced treatment of this controversial topic is provided by economist Sidney Weintraub:

> There is no intent ... to assert that multinational corporations invariably provide their workers with optimal working conditions and good salaries and are always careful to avoid environmental degradation ... . We also know that wages and working conditions in foreign transplants generally are superior to those of domestic enterprises.[43]

---

41. S. Prakash Sethi, Murray Weidenbaum, and Paul McCleary, "A Case Study of Independent Monitoring of U.S. Overseas Production," *Global Focus*, vol. 12, no. 1 (2000), pp. 142–143.

42. Ibid., pp. 150–151. For a broader view, see Erin Burnett and James Mahan Jr., "Monitoring Compliance With International Labor Standards," *Challenge*, March–April 2001 p. 51–72.

43. Sidney Weintraub, "Critical Aspects of the Global Economy," *Issues in International Political Economy*, November 2000, p. 3. For a less optimistic assessment, see Sam Dillon, "Profits Raise Pressure on Border Factories," *New York Times*, February 15, 2001, p. 1 *et ff*.

A similar upbeat assessment was provided by Morton Halpern, at the time a member of the Clinton administration's National Security Council staff: "There is no question that U.S. business can and does play a positive and important role in promoting the openness of societies, prosperity, environmental protection, and the setting of high standards for business practices generally."[44]

The issue of improving labor and environmental standards can be viewed in a broader context. Almost by definition, poor countries lack the capability to finance their own economic development on a large scale. During much of the nineteenth century, European investors financed many of America's canals, railroads, steel mills, and other essentials for becoming an industrialized nation. One may wonder where the United States would be today if Europe in the nineteenth century had been as suspicious of economic development as some interest groups are today.

It is instructive, in this regard, to consider a more recent experience. In 1996, Intel, the world's largest semiconductor producer, built an assembly and test plant in Costa Rica. In the factory's first full year of operation, Costa Rica's gross domestic product increased by 8.4 percent, the Intel production accounting for a substantial share of the nation's growth. The wage level rose since the plant's 2000 employees were paid an average of $5,000 a year, considerably above the nations' per capita income of $3,200.[45]

* * *

It is most unlikely that all the areas of disagreement on international trade and globalization can be quickly resolved. However, some creativity may help in starting the difficult but necessary process of achieving common ground. In that spirit, the following section presents a variety of proposals that should have some appeal to the contending camps.

Realistically, no side in the trade debate should be expected to yield on what they consider to be matters of basic principle. However, we ought to be able to identify a set of initial, albeit modest, actions that appeal to both sides. There could be a long-term benefit from this limited, incremental approach. It could help to restore a degree of trust on the part of the contending forces. A dialogue on these proposals would set in motion a process that could provide each side with a better understanding of the other. History provides a warning. The decline of globalization and open markets following World War I was due, at least in part, to the rising concerns over their unaddressed negative aspects.[46]

44. "Clinton Administration Encourages Voluntary Business Code," *ILO Washington Focus*, Summer 1995, p. 8.

45. Joseph P. Quinlan and Andrea L. Prochniak, "The Asymmetry of FDI Flows to the Developing Nations," *Morgan Stanley Dean Witter Global Insights*, February 12, 2001, p. 1.

46. Jeffrey Williamson, *Globalization and Inequality*, NBER Working Paper No. 5491 (Cambridge, Mass.: National Bureau of Economic Research, 1996), p. 20 (cited in Rodrik, *Globalization*, p. 8).

Identifying Common Ground

This report is not designed to provide a panacea for the economic problems, domestic or international, facing the United States. Rather, the proposals presented below are intended merely to start the difficult but necessary process of bridging the gap between the major antagonists in international trade policymaking. In an effort to be practical, the emphasis is on specific actions—rather than on trying to convince people of the errors in their positions.

Ways to Increase the Benefits of Trade Policy

A good start would be to act on some of the serious criticisms of existing trade policies. The concern over the lack of fairness in trade rules and procedures is often justified, even if the response in the form of trade restriction may not be. The following five suggestions are designed to respond positively without diminishing the continuing effort to reduce barriers to international commerce.

1. *The United States should adopt a tougher position on trade issues.* Promoting free trade is not just a matter of opening our markets to the products of other nations. Those nations need to do a better job of opening their markets to our products. Free trade, properly conducted, is a two-way street. Foreign trade barriers offend the sense of fairness of Americans who see the greater openness of our economy.

2. *The United States should strengthen its efforts to monitor and enforce trade agreements.* We need to take those agreements more seriously. Responsibility for enforcement should be elevated within the two trade policy agencies, the Department of Commerce and the Office of the U.S. Trade Representative. Sufficient numbers of highly qualified staff should be assigned to this task, which is not now the case. The budgets for trade agreement enforcement should be increased accordingly.

3. *The United States should work harder to get the nations we trade with to fully enforce the trade agreements they have entered into.* Signing an agreement to open borders to the products of other countries is an important step. It needs to be followed by action to carry out those commitments. Sadly, this has not always been true. For example, at times China has responded to a commitment to eliminate some paperwork obstacle to imports by substituting a new paperwork burden.

4. *WTO procedures should be made more transparent.* Some of the procedural proposals of the environmental and labor groups are sound and should be

supported. The call by the Sierra Club and the National Wildlife Federation for "transparency and accountability" in trade policy is both sensible and constructive.[47] The WTO should become far more open than it has been. The general sessions of trade negotiations, where countries are setting out their basic positions, should be open to the public. That would be comparable to the operations of the U.S. Congress. With the fewest of exceptions, each chamber holds its sessions in public and most of the committee hearings (except for national security) are also open. Executive sessions, where the serious bargaining goes on, remain closed. This is an effective division of labor. Compromises are going to be crafted in private. If the formal rules do not permit the organization to hold such private sessions, then the real decisionmaking will shift to less-efficient informal encounters.

A greater array of interest groups should be allowed to present their views without converting the WTO into an ineffective debating society. A similar suggestion has been made to open up the relatively closed process of developing and carrying out U.S. trade policy. Some urge that the way that trade agreements are negotiated should be changed to include more public assessments of their likely impacts and more consultation on the part of the executive branch with members of Congress and key interest groups.[48]

The WTO could also benefit from a variety of organizational improvements. The following changes in the organization's vital dispute settlement process have been suggested by trade policy experts:

- Allow parties who have an interest in the case to participate in a proceeding as a "friend of the court."

- Weed out cases that lack merit by improving the rules governing "preliminary rulings."

- Because developing the list of potential members of each dispute panel is difficult and time consuming, establish a permanent roster of potential panelists.

- Provide procedures for the appeals body to send a case back to the panel ("remanding" it).

- Open panel hearings to government and nongovernment observers, as courts typically do. This does not require that the panel deliberations be public events.

- Set time limits for distributing summaries of briefs. Such action would enhance the public's knowledge of the issues.[49]

5. *The United States should reduce the self-inflicted wounds on its own export efforts.* The Cold War is over and so is the justification for much of our export restric-

---

47. See Destler and Balint, *The New Politics,* p. 37.
48. Trade Deficit Review Commission, *The Trade Deficit,* p. 201.
49. Trade Deficit Review Commission, *The Trade Deficit,* pp. 216–217.

tions. Specifically, we should relax export controls on the technologies with both defense and civilian uses. Where U.S. producers do not have a monopoly on a particular technology, export controls are futile. Producers in other nations can deliver the same technology or product without the handicaps imposed on U.S. companies.

Export sanctions should be limited to those cases where a vital national interest is clearly at stake *and* where the likelihood of effectiveness is high. Few proposed sanctions would meet such a simple test.

6. *The United States should modernize its own trade protection legislation.* As a practical manner, the antidumping statute has become counterproductive to U.S. interests. In order to take a strong position on opening trade overseas, we must promptly clean up the deficiencies in our own international trade policies. We can begin by eliminating the antidumping approach in favor of the more enlightened "escape" clause in existing trade legislation, whereby the various interests affected are balanced more carefully and special-interest pressures more readily contained.

Ways to Reduce the Costs of Trade Policy

An effective international trade policy for the United States must go beyond opening markets. In order to win the support of skeptical Americans, such a policy should also reduce the costs that are imposed on specific groups in our society.

1. *The United States must respond more fully to the concerns of the people hurt by globalization.* The most enthusiastic proponent of globalization and free trade must acknowledge that these forces generate costs as well as benefits. To avoid setting up an inefficient and ineffective welfare program, policymakers must take great care in designing a sensible response. The focus of U.S. worker adjustment policy should be on positive approaches that help more people participate in economic growth, rather than providing relief from or seeking to halt economic change. In the short run, the effectiveness of the existing trade adjustment programs should be enhanced by simplifying the bureaucratic structure that has developed. Combining the general Trade Adjustment Assistance Program with the special NAFTA adjustment program would surely help.

2. *The most fundamental aspect of an effective worker assistance policy is to do a much better job of educating and training Americans to become more productive and higher-wage members of the nation's workforce.* A more productive work force is the key to long-term international competitiveness. For younger workers, the emphasis should be on training and education. Here, more attention deserves to be given to junior colleges, an often-overlooked part of the nation's educational system. Many of these community-oriented institutions of learning are now organized especially to meet the needs of displaced workers, including those who need to brush up on their basic language and math skills. In some

cases, these community colleges help people launch new businesses, especially in areas where traditional manufacturing is declining.

3. *The increased concern about those hurt by trade must extend to older workers.* We must be candid in acknowledging that often, although not always, the adjustment challenge is far more difficult for older workers than for younger people. Unemployed 50-year-old factory workers have little incentive to train for jobs at pay lower and in competition with people half their age. Consideration should be given to the proposals for a new system of wage insurance to compensate unemployed workers for taking jobs at lower pay than their customary work, and to do so promptly before their skills become rusty.[50] However, the experience with government-sponsored income maintenance programs has been very mixed. The late 1990s demonstrated that the most effective job-loss adjustment program is a growing economy creating new jobs as a rapid rate.

4. *The United States should take the lead in developing a constructive alternative response to the demand for directly linking labor standards with trade agreements.* In view of the strong public support for such linkage, it is unrealistic to "just say no." That support extends far beyond the limited ranks of organized labor. Many citizens are uncomfortable with the vision of child labor in Honduras displacing adult workers in South Carolina.[51] Nevertheless, trying to impose costly standards on unwilling developing countries, as was demonstrated at the Seattle meetings of the WTO, will only force them to oppose a new round of multilateral trade negotiations. But it certainly is not adequate to respond merely by taking the position that labor standards are more appropriately handled by the International Labor Organization.

In order for that latter position to be credible, the United States must show much stronger support for the ILO's existing initiatives than it has so far. Congress should promptly approve all of the core labor standards promulgated by the ILO in 1998. After all, the United States does favor the essential elements— freedom from forced labor, effective abolition of child labor, nondiscrimination in employment, and effective recognition of the right to collective bargaining. Why make an issue of supporting policies that our Congress has consistently voted for over the years? Rather, a positive response would be for the United States to take the lead in urging the ILO to set up a communications process using the Internet to inform consumers around the world of the producers who violate the core standards.

In addition, the United States should continue to support the special ILO program to help poor families whose children are taken off factory employment and to get the youngsters back to school.[52]

---

50. Burtless et al., *Globaphobia*, pp. 143–145.
51. Rodrik, *Globalization*, p. 5.
52. "Responding to Seattle: Interview with Jagdish Bhagwati," *Challenge*, vol. 44, no. 1, January–February 2001, p. 12.

The WTO rule allowing member nations to ban imports of goods produced using prison labor (Article XX) should be expanded to cover other forms of forced labor, notably forced child labor. The WTO could declare that forced labor violates fundamental market principles, thus providing a rationale for its limited involvement in labor standards.

5. *The United States should support trading rules that are more environmentally friendly.* Trade officials often have a "tin ear" when it comes to dealing with related public policy issues, especially environmental. A single action by the WTO—declaring that the U.S. ban on importing tuna caught in ways that harms dolphins violates WTO rules—energized vehement opposition by the environmental movement.[53]

Priority should be given to liberalizing trade in environmental goods and services. It is of mutual benefit that the developing countries acquire the environmental cleanup capabilities of the advanced developed nations. In addition, Article XX exceptions could be expanded to provide "safe harbors" for trade actions consistent with provisions of multilateral environmental agreements. Thus, the United States and other nations could be allowed to protect endangered species, but not to do so unilaterally.

* * *

Time is not necessarily on the side of maintaining the status quo in U.S. international trade policy. While the absence of fast-track legislation inhibits U.S. trade negotiators, the European Union is strengthening its commercial ties with Latin America.

Nevertheless, hopes should not be raised too high for the achievement of any quick breakthrough in U.S. policy on international trade until a feeling of trust or at least common understanding is achieved between proponents of open trade and those with other priorities. Adoption of some of the suggestions made here would help reduce the gap between the two groups.

One modest change would be to moderate the vocabularies of the two camps so that the debates are not apparently being carried on between "environmental whackos" and "greedy monopolists." This is a situation where "voluntary standards" would help!

---

53. For details, see Dorothy J. Black, "International Trade v. Environmental Protection: The Case of the U.S. Embargo on Mexican Tuna," *Law and Policy in International Business*, vol. 24 (1), Fall 1992, pp. 123–152.

About the Author

Murray Weidenbaum has been an economist in three worlds—business, government, and academia. At the time of this writing, he is a distinguished visiting scholar at CSIS, as well as a member of the CSIS Board of Trustees. He holds the Mallinckrodt Distinguished University Professorship at Washington University in St. Louis, where he also serves as honorary chairman of the university's Weidenbaum Center on the Economy, Government, and Public Policy. In 1981 and 1982, Dr. Weidenbaum was President Reagan's first chairman of the Council of Economic Advisers. From 1983 to 1989, he was a member of the President's Economic Policy Advisory Board. Earlier, Dr. Weidenbaum was the assistant secretary of the treasury for economic policy in the Nixon administration. He also served as the corporate economist at the Boeing Company. He is a member of the boards of directors of Harbour Group, Macroeconomic Advisers, and Tesoro Petroleum Corporation. He is a member of the advisory boards of the Center for Strategic Tax Reform, American Council for Capital Formation, American Enterprise Institute, and Foreign Policy Research Institute. He received a B.B.A. from City College of New York, an M.A. from Columbia University, and a Ph.D. from Princeton University. He has been a faculty member at Washington University since 1964 and was the chairman of the Economics Department from 1966 to 1969. He is the author of eight books, including *Business and Government in the Global Marketplace* (sixth edition, 1999), *The Bamboo Network* (1996), and *Small Wars, Big Defense* (1992).